Ever After

Brenda Jenkyns

Illustrations by
Kathy Garren

BMJ Publishing

ISBN-13: 978-1481093897

ISBN-10: 1481093894

Calgary, Alberta, Canada

(403) 818-7520

For Prince, Paris and Blanket

and for Katherine

with love,

BJ & KG

Thank you Michael, for always giving us your best

Once there was a little boy
who loved to dance and sing.
He danced before he could walk
and he sang before he could talk.
The music he heard in his head
and all around him was so beautiful,
it flowed right out of him
and into the world.

The little boy lived with his parents
and eight brothers and sisters
in a small house. The father worked hard
at a steel mill every day and, on most
evenings, the family gathered
in the living room to sing together.

The parents were happy to have
their children home,
where they knew they were safe.

One day, the father was late coming home. When he arrived, he was holding a shiny new guitar. The children were excited, but their mother knew the family needed many other things, much more than they needed a guitar. She also knew that her husband had a dream. His dream was that, through music, their children would have a chance at a better life, one that might otherwise not be possible for them.

The boys in the family began to practice
playing music together every day.
The father was very strict and expected
a lot from his sons. The little boy danced
and sang right along with his older
brothers. With his beautiful voice,
he soon became the lead singer of the group.

The little house was bursting with music.

When the father knew they were ready,

he entered his sons in a talent contest - they won.

Over time, they won more contests,

and were soon playing at parties and nightclubs

almost every night.

Someone from a record company

saw the boys perform and asked them

to make a record. This was the chance

the father had been waiting for.

Before long, the family moved

to California and the

group began to enjoy the success

their father had imagined.

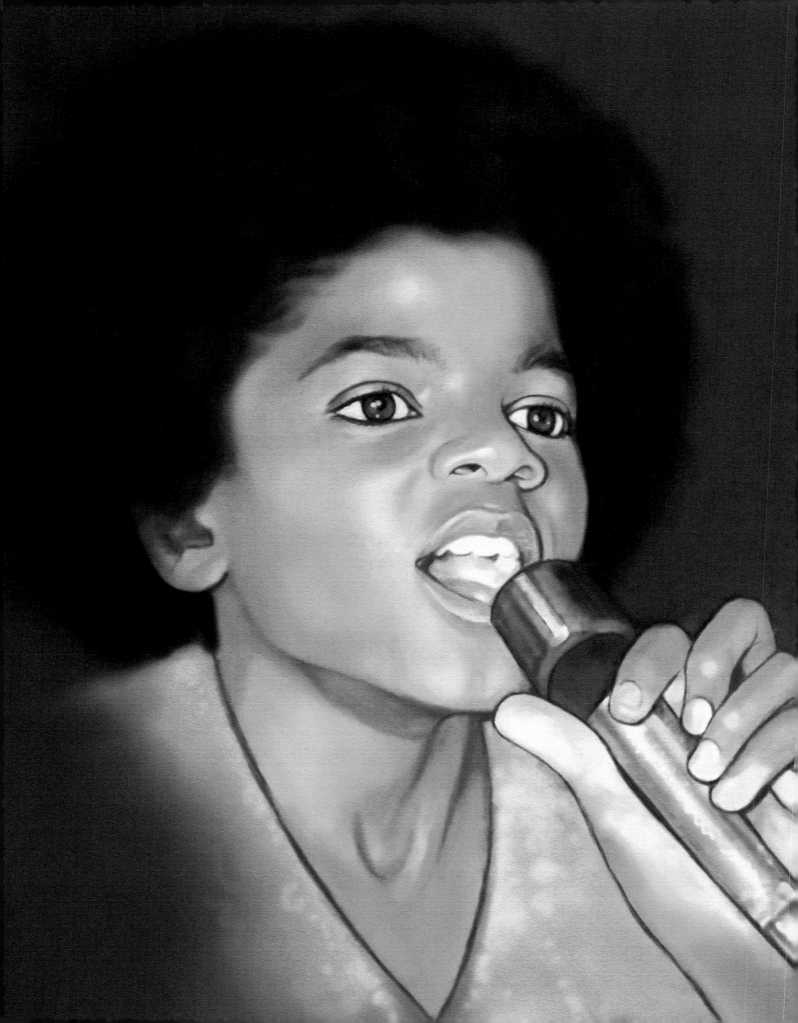

The little boy was totally comfortable

and confident while performing and

seemed much older than his ten years.

When he sang and danced,

he put everything he had into every song.

He sometimes felt as if he had become the music.

By the time he was twelve years old,

he and his brothers had recorded

four hit records.

Although he loved performing,

the little boy often wished he could be a kid

like any other. He saw children playing

in the park across the street from where he

went to rehearse after his lessons each day.

He could not join them because

his job was to record music.

This made him feel sad.

Even though he was now

well known as a child singer,

he was lonely.

The boy knew in his heart that his talents

were a gift of nature, meant for him

to share with the world. He thought,

by doing his best at expressing his gifts,

he could help others to find theirs.

He began to branch away from the family

group to write and sing his own songs.

He was a perfectionist and, when his music

was recorded the way he heard it in his head,

the results were amazing. His songs became

the biggest hits ever, and he became

the biggest star ever.

Although he was happy with the success of his music, being famous meant he could not be like other people. Simple things, such as shopping or going to a movie, were no longer easy. People crowded around him wherever he went, trying to touch him and ask for his autograph. Except when he was performing, the boy spent much of his time with windows separating him from the rest of the world.

People loved the boy for his music, but he also wanted to be loved
for the person he was inside. He found it was children he could
trust to always be natural and honest.
They liked him for himself and were not impressed by fame.
They just wanted to have fun, and so did he.

The boy spent his childhood in an adult world.
When he grew up, he never stopped enjoying
childlike things like a good
water balloon fight, climbing
trees and watching cartoons.

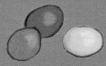

He bought a ranch and filled it with everything

he had not been able to enjoy in his childhood.

There was an amusement park, video arcade,

zoo, theatre and a candy and ice cream shop.

He invited sick and underprivileged children

to his ranch to enjoy a day of fun. Because

of his own lack of a normal childhood, he felt

the pain of all children who were not able to

enjoy theirs. He visited hospitals and orphanages

all over the world and gave millions of dollars

to charity, to help children.

His fans appreciated his gentle, loving and humble nature, as much as his amazing talent. They showed him never ending loyalty and support over a lifetime of entertaining. The boy expressed his love for his fans by doing his best for them, musically and creatively. With each new project he challenged himself to create what had never been done before. His example inspired people to be the best they could be, at whatever they loved to do.

The boy had become a man and was proud of his work. He had three children of his own and was devoted to being a good father to them.

He taught them that they could do anything in life, if they wanted it enough and were willing to work hard.

He made sure they had every chance to enjoy their childhood, and he told them every day how much he loved them.

The boy had done
what he had always been
inspired to do,

sing,

dance,

and make a difference.

The music, the memories
and the message,
will live on in love,

ever after

If Michael has made a difference
in your life, tell us about it at
www.michaeljacksoneverafter.com
We'd love to hear your story.